Holsteins and Rattlesnakes and Geckos, Oh My!

by

Ron J. Woelfel

authorHOUSE

1663 LIBERTY DRIVE, SUITE 200
BLOOMINGTON, INDIANA 47403
(800) 839-8640
www.authorhouse.com

First published by AuthorHouse 08/03/04

ISBN: 1-4184-8241-2 (sc)

Library of Congress Control Number:2004095431

Printed in the United States of America
Bloomington, Indiana

This book is printed on acid-free paper.

This book is a composition of non-fictional chronological events through my life from day one until it was time to document my happenings before it was too late.

ACKNOWLEDGEMENTS

*A*ll of my family was taken into account as well as many of my dear friends and co-workers. I regret that not everyone I have come to appreciate in life is mentioned, but each one is not forgotten. Special thanks to my parents Linus and RoseMary, for making this wonderful journey possible, my sisters Dori Schmitz for the book cover design and Kathy Arndt for job of proofing, my teachers who were very instrumental in their task of keeping me on the right track, the doctors and nurses that helped me over the speed bumps.

FOREWORD

*A*utobiography is literally a chronicle of one's life written by the subject. My communication may not always be clear but hopefully you'll get my meaning nonetheless.

The saga of my life's adventures started when I was incredibly young.

CHAPTER I

MY LIFE STARTED AT THE VERY BEGINNING

I'm told it was a cold trip to St. Agnes Hospital in Fond du Lac, Wisconsin which is approximately 25 miles from Chilton. I thought it was rather nice where I was, but I needed to get out of there because I had places to go and things to do. Even though my dad (in the military) was nowhere around for the trip to the hospital, that was no reason for me to stay where I was. If I remember right, I told mom, "I'm getting out of here" and just like that, there I was at 6:53 pm on Friday, November 16th 1945. Of course, a guy by the name of, Doctor J.J. Minahan was there as a spectator. I figured it was a miracle that I made it this far but, there was much further to go. I kept asking mom, "Is it time to go home yet?" She insisted "Be a little patient." Well, I was 'little' but I never did understand that other word. My trip home was delayed an extra day because

Grandpa Bill couldn't get through the deep snow that had fallen. Sure enough, that's the way my life started. I had lots of things planned already.

Anyhow, mom wasn't taking any chances, so I was baptized barely two weeks after I came into this world. She figured, better now when I can't fight back yet, because there was no way I was going to let them pour that cold water over my head later. And besides, the crucial game wasn't even started yet. Mom and dad appointed my Uncle Joseph and Aunt Apolonia to take over if they couldn't handle me any more. They called them baptismal sponsors, but I knew better what the purpose was. It would take four grownups to watch over me. I spent my first 7 months with mom at my maternal grandparent's house and then relocated to the homestead farm two miles south when dad arrived back from WWII.

Homestead

Later on in my early years, an event that always stands out in my mind took place in the summer of 1949. The family, mom, dad, Jim (my older brother), Kathleen, Eunice (younger sisters) and I went to visit a bedridden Great Uncle by the name of Herman in

Rockville, Wisconsin. This guy in bed reached over, took my arm and slowly pulled me towards him. That really put some fear into me. I didn't know where he was going, but I was quite sure I didn't want to go with him even if there was candy there. This memory is something that has stayed with me over the years though I couldn't remember the year or date until I was informed by my parents of that time.

It was now the start of many mischievous years. Always having that knack for what makes things go, my friend, I'll call Butch who was about 3 years old and I went out to the barn on the upper level where we had our new Ford tractor sitting just waiting for attention. Well, between the two of us, we figured, well what did we figure? So, something told us no harm can come to us for sitting on the tractor, so we did. That got to be boring after a while. I saw dad just push down on this little button next to the shifter and the tractor moves. Well, the Ford was in a high gear so luckily it didn't start, but it did move forward as long as the button was held down. We got it to move about 6 feet forward when our guardian angels took over and told us we better stop. We had only a few more feet to go from the back of the barn and then a 12 foot drop straight down. I guess He wanted us around a little longer because there would be more lessons to learn. The chicken coop was another popular hangout for Butch to visit and that would result in the egg supply taking a major hit. I believe the chickens were always glad when he left. I think they knew I would never do mischief like that on my own.

One particular trip to grandma's house with my dad had an undesirable end result. He had told me to wait in the car because he would be right back, so that was fine for about one and a half minutes or until he got in the house. I quickly got out of the backseat of the car and slammed the door shut. Oh, but wait, I forgot to take my little finger out of the way. That caused some pain. I let out a scream which brought Aunt Germaine running out of the house to see what the commotion was about. We had a 1951 Chevy which was much more structurally sound than the cars of today. That Chevy door wouldn't let go of my finger until she open it, grabbed me and took me into the house to wash off the blood. My dad then took me to the doctor to patch up the damage. The car survived without a scratch. Another lesson learned......when I was told to wait in the car......that meant, 'wait in the car except for an emergency'. I thought it was an emergency. Grandpa always had peppermint candy in one of his old cigar boxes for poor starving grandkids. But, life has a way of telling us to be respectful of the person in charge.

CHAPTER II

THE WONDERS OF ELEMENTARY

Well, mom said it was time to go to school come September of '51, but she would have said anything to get me out of the house for the day. This was just a little country catholic elementary school consisting of grades 1 thru 8 with the 4 lower grades in one room and 4 upper grades in another room. It was the same school my dad and grandpa attended and maybe even my great grandpa. The rooms were named, Little Room for the lower grades and Big Room for the upper, but the size of the rooms was just the opposite of what they were called. Anyway, maybe it was because of the grades located there. It started out with two nuns for the lower and one nun for the upper grades. Later on in my school days I guess when I was in the Big Room, they figured they could manage the young kids with just one nun. Since it was just an old-fashioned two room school, we didn't have any indoor restrooms. We needed to be excused to go outside to use the outhouse. In winter it seemed like a two mile walk. Sometimes I just got frozen to that hole in the board and it took a little longer than it should have. But there were so many things to see and do there. During the warmer days it took slightly longer and the diversions were more plentiful. It was always time away from class while the clock kept on ticking. Soon it would be time to go home again where there were always obligations like going fishing, playing with the dog or just hanging out with some new litter of kittens.

For some anomalous reason in 4th grade, I always ended up in the front of the classroom on the floor to do my homework for reasons baffling to me at that time. Maybe, I thought, that's the way school is supposed to be and I was always getting a reward for something. I remember a classmate by the name of Mary, told the teacher, "Maybe the reason for not getting his homework done was because I was left-handed". It made sense to me! But the teacher didn't agree. I guess Mary had never seen someone left-handed before, so she just determined that was the source of my problem.

During the summer in between crops, it was one of those get-away-weekends, that mom and dad decided they needed some time away from my older brother and younger sisters, but not me. They hired a babysitter who happened to be a distant cousin named Stella. She babysat several times before and I guess she was dependable. Also it was the time when my parents had hired a contractor to dig out for a basement under the laundry room in the house. It was a project lasting several weeks and mom always told us kids to stay out of their way in the basement. Larry (younger brother), who was 2 years old at the time, was always trying to crawl in that new hole that they were digging. The job involved knocking out a doorway in a 20 inch thick concrete wall between the present basement and the part being dug out.

It was an intense and thunderous sound from an air hammer being used and just the sound was enough to scare me. Stella didn't think it was so bad, so to get my brother and me out of her hair, she sent us down in the basement to watch the guys work. We both knew she just wanted to call her boyfriend from up the road. That didn't sit well for us after a little while, so we came back upstairs crying. The next day when mom and dad came home we couldn't wait to tell them what Stella made us do. Because dad heard it from both of us, he reckoned we were telling the truth and she was in need of some reprimanding. He took her outside to a faucet located on a house wall about 4 feet up from the ground and held her head under cool running water for what seemed like a half minute. Seeing this made us giggle just around the corner. Then that noise in the basement didn't seem so loud after all. I remember asking dad if he was washing her hair or if she needed to be baptized. I don't remember if that was the last babysitting assignment with us or not. It might have been because there was Leona shortly after that and she was good at breaking yardsticks on me. In those days they were made of much harder wood than the modern ones of today. Maybe that's why they broke. The county fair was only held once a year so I had to be good sometimes to make the supply of those sticks last until they could be replenished.

CHAPTER III

ORIGIN OF THE WIDE SPOT

We needed something for excitement when we had no field work. We used the small stream a half mile from home for our so-called swimming hole. This place was wider than the rest of the creek so we had no name for it other than the Wide Spot. We called it swimming though the water was only a foot and a half deep. We thought we had to improve conditions so Jim took the tractor with the front loader one day and formed a dam to increase the depth. Now we had four feet of water and almost deep enough to dive in. Many hours were spent there whenever conditions were not ideal for the field work. We could only spend 15 minutes or so in the water and then come out to take the bloodsuckers out from between our toes.

For a couple years, it was necessary to spend a week to ten days down in Milwaukee with my friend Butch and his family. This was a big city for me. This farm boy needed some training in what troubles were available. I usually accompanied him on his daily paper route and how I ever survived that with all the cars I'll never know. I never experienced driving a bike in traffic. Butch didn't care or didn't realize my lack of experience riding a bike in the city. It seemed in those days, drivers respected kids on bikes. I remember hearing brakes on more than one occasion. The week of the state fair was especially exciting because we always got into the fair free to sell newspapers. The sooner they were sold, the sooner we could do what interested us. We had our regulars. They helped build our business but by the time we had discovered outlets for our paper supply, the fair was usually over.

It was an annual event to make at least one journey to Milwaukee, approximately 80 miles, to see a major league baseball game during the summer. Those were the years of the Milwaukee Braves and collecting baseball cards. Ones not in high demand were used to add sound effects to my bike. It was in 1957 that the Braves were in the World Series. I never missed a game on the radio throughout the season. I didn't have much else to occupy my evenings prior to television. Homework was not a top priority. Because the Braves were in the World Series, we had to see them in action. We as a family went two miles to our Uncle Victor's house to watch them on television. Not too many people had a TV at that time. This was quite amazing to watch them even in black and white. I remember dad saying "if the Braves are in the series again next year, we will have our own television". Well these guys were good, so in 1958 they were in the series again and we got our 1st television. To see Aaron, Mathews, Adcock, Spahn and my other idols on television was a major breakthrough in technology for me.

A summer time activity to keep me occupied and generate somewhat of an income was raising rabbits, literally by the hundreds. I couldn't keep up making cages for them. Soon I was putting them in a big make shift fenced area in the apple orchard. This idea didn't last long because now there were many more. I started selling them to a meat market toward the end of summer and kept about a dozen over winter in the unoccupied pig barn. They were kept in a one room area 20 feet square and usually by the next spring, ended up with a few more to relocate outside again. After I started high school, I realized the reason I kept getting more and more of them. It was then I decided to rid myself of that business and devote more time to preferable hobbies like fishing. Helping with milking the cows usually took precedence before my rabbits. My pet Holstein cow was "tootsie". She allowed me to ride on her back when coming home from the pasture. But my favorite was actually a black cow at A&W.

A phenomenon that always took place during the summer was the acre of pickles dad planted for us kids to maintain and harvest. Every two days for 8 weeks they needed to be harvested and delivered to the processing plant in Chilton. There they were sorted according to size. It was supposed to be a revenue generating project for us, but really it was to protect us against boredom.

It was in this time of life when I was able to take my first ride in an airplane. A municipal airport was built in New Holstein circa 1958 and dad was anxious to see what our farm looked like from up there in the sky. It was also at the time when we received the Century Farm Family Ownership award so the ride had special significance. Dad, Jim and I, accompanied by a pilot of course, took a 30 minute flight over the surrounding area which included our farm. And this was more exciting than the county fair. At the time, I don't think it cost much over $10 for the 3 of us.

CHAPTER IV

ADAPTATION AFTER ELEMENTARY

Well, it was time by 1959 to get out of this elementary stuff and reposition myself into high school. The Friday before formal 8th grade graduation, for some preposterous reason, our teacher thought we needed rehearsal with our march down the aisle in church. That being the last day of school, I got to take my bike to school. The weather was great. My buddy, Joe was always getting me in trouble, knowing good well I would never have thought of doing these things alone. We agreed that practice was completely pointless. We had things of much greater importance to do. As the school day was winding down, our sense of duty was getting wound up. We were outdoors for the last recess, Joe and I hopped on our bikes and rode to his house in a little village called Hayton 2 miles away. There we were greeted by Joe's mom. She was told, "School let out early because it was the last day". It made sense to us. So we just messed around in the auto junk yard behind his place for an hour or two chasing wild cats. Since it was getting time for school to let out we headed back and found most of the other kids had left. I was informed in a not-so-happy manner that I was missed in the graduation rehearsal. I don't know why, because there were seven of us in the class so how would she miss just one. I awoke that graduation Sunday morning with very painful enlargement of my salivary glands, otherwise know as the mumps. There was no graduation ceremony for me. Now when I look back at the missed practice on Friday, why waste my precious time doing something of no benefit. Don't tell me things happen for no reason!

Activity was kind of normal that summer with considerable time spent with neighbor Alfred and buddy Joe. I guess we were getting educated in things not taught in school, especially elementary school. Because of the farm, the only days with free time were when it rained. What can a person do when it rains? It posed a challenge but somehow I always managed. I was able to generate some income by assisting dad with his custom work helping neighbors with their harvesting. This is how I saved up enough money to buy my very own 16 gauge shotgun, a used Winchester Model 12 pump action and was I ever proud of it. My hunting buddies were a neighbor Alfred and Joe from Hayton.

The thought of high school was somewhat worrisome because I didn't know how much time it would take away from the imperative activities that I felt I needed to accomplish. My older brother had been to this school the previous year. He clued me in on some things to be aware of......like girls. From what I could tell, they meant nothing but complexity in one's life. So at that point, I determined they would be too much interference with hunting and fishing. Also, most girls didn't smoke at that age so, that was another reason not to interconnect with them.

The start of high school in 1959 was not as expected. They didn't teach the things I wanted to know about, like how to build a raft to use on the creek during spring thaw and a proven way to stalk that big elusive buck during hunting season. A week or so into my freshman year it came to initiation day for all of us newcomers. The sophomores were waiting for this day. All the freshmen boys were taken into the shower room one by one for a fully clothed shower. There were only eight of us and because my brother was a sophomore, I didn't get to go. Somehow, I felt neglected or honored. I'm not sure which.

In my 2nd year as a sophomore, things started opening up for me. I thought I might as well make the best of my situation because there are 3 more years to go. This year I got to initiate the freshmen, even though I didn't know why I had to help because of my non-participation the year before.

CHAPTER V

TOUGH YEARS AHEAD

This would be my last year in high school. Then I could get on with my life. It started out with me getting assigned to a front row seat in the school bus only because someone from the upper elementary class complained that I was always picking on him. The bus company and the principal decided it was in the best interest of all except me of course. When class elections were held, for some unknown reason I was elected to the student council. That only lasted for a few weeks. I guess maybe because of lack of interest or enthusiasm. I was on long enough to help plan an autumn hay ride in October for the juniors and seniors. It started out as a fun-filled evening until one of my classmates fell off the front of the wagon and was fatally injured when she was run over by the two wagons in tow. We used all resources to revive her but to no avail. Because we were several miles away from the nearest phone we flagged down a passerby for help. Even if we would have had immediate response, Donna would not come back. We all went through some sad times at school. We only had 16 in our class so it was like we lost a family member. She was a second cousin to me and was slated to be our valedictorian in the graduating class of 1963.

Later that month of October while in Physical Education class during indoor soccer I ran into one of the underclassmen that were probably a good 100 pounds heavier than me. His feet were firmly planted and it was like running into a wall. He never budged and I just fell over backwards and hit my head on the gym floor. Not wanting to be embarrassed, I quickly rolled over, shook my head, sprang to my feet and continued playing. I remember for an instant those little white stars circling over my head. They were soon a thing of the past and now I acquired respect for bigger underclassmen.

Things were rather fine for a week or two and then something started going awry with my feelings and other body motions. It was too coincidental to account for happenings after that. Although my doctor at the time said the evidence was inconclusive. My writing was deteriorating and my left side was going numb along with other cerebral disturbances. Soon my teachers started noticing unconventional behavior and brought it to my attention. I always figured it would go away in due time until things at home were also noticed by my superiors, meaning mom and dad. By the end of November, it was something that needed attention, so mom and dad scheduled me for a doctor's visit. The doc looked into my eyes with one of those funny looking lights and immediately recommended further evaluation by a neurologist at Wisconsin University Hospital in Madison. I was admitted on the last Thursday of November and released on Christmas Eve with mom and dad making many trips to Madison. This was an extreme hardship on my parents being over 100 miles from home. Plus they had six other siblings at home to feed, all younger than me with Nancy being the youngest at 5 months.

After 4 days of extensive testing, they located the problem but did not clue me in on any details. This testing all started on a Thursday and I phoned my neighbor friend Alfred informing him I would probably be home by Friday so we could go hunting. By Monday, mom and dad were informed of the situation. I was in surgery on Tuesday December 4th. My doctor probably figured, the less I know about what's about to happen, the better for me. And besides, I was under 18 years of age, so what did I have to say? I would have told them, I can live with it. A neurosurgeon removed a small tumor from somewhere on the upper left side of my cerebrum. This was the cause of my equilibrium going off course and other physical disorders. The remainder of my stay was less than desirable and I would rather have been in school, even knowing my discontent for school.

Over the 3 weeks before my discharge I did get to know a male nurse. Ralph was an orderly assigned to my care when heavy moving or lifting was required. At one time early in the evening after his shift, he went home and came back with one of his 4 week old cocker spaniel puppies wrapped in a hospital gown and brought it up to my 4th floor room. My eyes lit up like they never had since I left home and I got to hold him like I never wanted to leave him go. I told Ralph I definitely want to buy him. I paid him $10 and named him "Ralph". That dog turned out to be my best pal and hunting companion. He could flush out any pheasant, if there was one around when hunting and I know a girl friend couldn't or wouldn't do that for me. I was discharged on Christmas Eve. Though I was eager to get home, I didn't look forward to the long ride.

In January I was scheduled for cobalt radiation therapy for 5 weeks 5 days per week in Fond du Lac at St. Agnes Hospital as an outpatient. This was only 25 miles away but nonetheless a hardship for my parents to overcome. The treatments caused me to be very nauseated which resulted in extreme weight loss, going from 155 pounds down to 97 pounds in 4 months. I didn't even need Jenny Craig for help. For graduation in June, I tried to participate but needed more time to convalesce. There wasn't much I could do that summer to get into trouble.

When September came I felt it was time to make some money so I was hired by Hipke Canning Factory in New Holstein, our local food processing company. Dick, the owner of the company, whom I had met in the hospital in Madison because his mother was there remembered me and probably felt somewhat benevolent for me. This was my first bona fide job with an actual paycheck. The season was over in November when I then took a job at Wilberscheid mink Ranch also near New Holstein. That only lasted two days due to the physical aspect which I had to endure. After approximately 2 weeks of deer hunting, I needed something substantial for income as I needed to get settled with transportation needs.

An historical event happened at this time I will always remember. Our President JFK was assassinated in Dallas, Texas which I was informed of at a meeting place called the Redwood Bar. Starting in December, Chilton Metal Products filled my need for income until I was informed of a better opportunity for 35 cents more per hour at Tecumseh Products, New Holstein. (Their season slows for the summer in April so I was laid-off). Unemployment was fine for a week but I was told I needed to work for my paycheck so I tried to make it at Lake To Lake dairy plant in Kiel. That was also very physical and two days later I was looking again. This time I found what I needed in Chilton at Aluminum Specialty a manufacturer of aluminum cookware and coffee pots. During this demanding year I was able to save enough for a down payment on a used 1957 Pontiac Chieftain, my very own first car. Working there was fine until I was recalled at Tecumseh in September of 1965.

CHAPTER VI

BIG CITY LIFE

Now with my own wheels, I was beginning to get attracted to the opposite sex or maybe just a little more disenchanted with outdoor sports. Only to a slight extent because the wheels still had a priority for transportation to favorite fishing and hunting territory. One of those late night missions with the guys, we made a hunger stop at K&R, a local truck stop café where we were not always appreciated. In the booth which we sat in, I noticed something torn up in the ashtray. Well, as curious as I am usually, I thought it might be of interest so I took all the pieces home and assembled the puzzle. It turned out to be a voided check with an address of a female acquaintance, whom I had met once or twice. I carefully taped it back together and sent it to her without a return address. After allowing some time for delivery, I called and informed her of carelessness. She couldn't believe someone would actually spend the time to thoroughly examine those little tiny itsy bitsy pieces. That was an enticement to find out more about that strange guy. In 1966, Joanne and I started our 19 year escapade.

With the country building up our presence in Viet Nam, nearly every male over 18 years of age was summoned by the Federal government to appear for a military physical. At first I was a little excited because if all was ok, I would join the Air Force. That didn't happen and I was classified 4-F which in those days meant "Not available for any military duty at this time". So this tribulation got me to start thinking, do I want to do this factory work the rest of my life? No! It was at that time I signed up for a course in airline training because I did like the skies and I couldn't get in the Air Force.

I purchased my first new car, a 1965 Corvair Monza, in the spring of 1966 thereby needing to make a slight adjustment in driving because of lack of horsepower compared to my previous Pontiac. Home study kept me busy most of the time that winter and when I was laid off again in April, I was headed for Minneapolis at an airline training school. Toward the end of the term, several of us students were flown to Chicago O'Hare airport for an interview with Ozark Airlines. We flew round trip the same day in a DC3. Boy, this was alright I thought, as we had four stops along the way. Take offs and landings were always fun in those days. After completing our training, we had another interview scheduled with Continental Airlines in Denver, Colorado. That flight was on a 727 jet and was my first time flying in a jet. When we returned to

Chicago that same day I was informed of a position with Ozark Airlines which I willingly accepted. Now that required me to relocate in the big city of Chicago which I was somewhat apprehensive about. After all, I was just a country boy that had never been to such a big city much less live in one. But it was time to get acquainted with the rest of the world because we only have this one life to do it in.

When I did make up my mind, I found a one room apartment in Des Plaines on the Northwest side. It was only for a month because I was getting married by the end of June and then would need something a little bigger. In June I had moved into a place in Niles which as only five additional miles to work. Most of our weekends that we didn't drive back to Wisconsin we spent at the airport because it had so many things to do. By September we were both getting home sick and I resigned from Ozark to take a position back at Tecumseh in Wisconsin.

We found a nice 2 bedroom apartment in New Holstein where we lived for 1 year. During that time my first born son Brian came into this world and I never did find out where he came from. That was also the year the Green Bay Packers won the championship game in what was later named the Ice Bowl. I was never much of a football fan until Lombardi came to Green Bay. Then my interests in the Packers started and I have been following them ever since as an indoor spectator. When the apartment lease was up after one year, we moved to a country home for lower rent a mile south of town. That is where my daughter Brenda appeared out of nowhere. Finally in 1969, we started looking for something we could call our own. We bought an acre of land from my dad on the northeast corner of the farm and on it we placed a mobile home.

In June that year reading the Sunday paper one weekend, I discovered an ad for a free round trip to Lake Havasu City, Arizona for land investment. I checked into the deal further and attended a promotional meeting in Appleton. Two weeks later we took the opportunity to fly out. We hopped on a plane in Milwaukee Saturday morning with temps in the middle 50's and got off the plane in Arizona at 107 degrees. It felt so good. In the afternoon we attended another meeting, toured the city, had a good breakfast with them and came back on Sunday in time for work on Monday. We were not in the financial state to make an investment at that time so it was just a two day vacation. From that time, my aspiration was to live in the desert. There is could explore the desert with its venomous creatures like rattlesnakes.

By that time I was working at Arps Corporation in New Holstein where I spent the next 14 years. After a year living in our mobile home a garage was built on our lot, so now we had a place to start accumulating possessions we didn't really need otherwise known as junk.

CHAPTER VII

NEW HOME CONSTRUCTION

It was during the 70's I decided there was more to life than working in a factory. I started taking night classes in engineering to better myself at Arps and thereafter. During these years we also outgrew the mobile home we were in so, I started doing some research on alternate habitation. I sought after something unique and economical which in turn got me interested in a geodesic dome home. After viewing several existing homes of that type, the decision was made to go ahead and build. I began construction in June 1978 while living in the mobile home. By late winter it was finished enough so we could move into the basement of the partially completed dome.

Dome House

My time at Arps Corporation was accelerating to a higher level when they promoted me to the Industrial Engineering Department. I was shop chairman for the union at the time and thereby it would eliminate a thorn in the side for the management. This promotion required me to fly to Cincinnati to attend a one week workshop for time study. Many evenings were also spent going to night classes to further my education in the engineering field for the next several years. I car pooled with a co-worker for the 20 mile trip to a technical school in Cleveland. We always had to slow way down to 10 mph for some domestic geese that were on the road. On the way back home I made a dare to Dan that he couldn't grab one of those geese by the neck and pull it into the car. Well by the time we got to New Holstein my car was so full of goose droppings inside that we finally had to release the culprit in some back alley in town. The following week the local paper had a short editorial from the police department that a couple out on their evening stroll came through this alley and got goosed. The department just took it as a hoax until they saw the evidence. They were informed they could have the goose if no one claimed it within a week. We needed to prevent monotony going to night school.

It was a couple years later that a previous supervisor encouraged me to join him at a company in Kiel called Stoelting Brothers which I accepted after some indecision. This lasted only one year and then the business downsized due to economic conditions and I was out of work. My interest in taking engineering classes also made it easier to find a new position. While in Milwaukee for an interview in October 1982 the Milwaukee Brewers won the American League Championship and gained them entry into the World Series. Downtown Milwaukee rocked as the celebrating went on near my hotel room. I did take part in it for a short time. The following day after the interview, I was hired as an Industrial Engineer at Gilson Brothers Company in Plymouth, Wisconsin. That position was very gratifying and gave me an enormous amount of confidence in the engineering field. Frank, my supervisor informed me I had great potential and would find little trouble in getting a real bona fide job somewhere in a suitable climate.

In November of 1983, the family flew to Orlando for a much needed vacation touring the newly opened Epcot Center and Disney World. After several days, we drove to Cape Canaveral and enlisted in several tours to see what our space program is made of. I was astonished with the size of the space shuttle garage and other features. We returned to Orlando to spend the night. The next morning we headed out to Tampa to see Busch Gardens and other sights for two more days before heading back to the cold weather of Wisconsin.

CHAPTER VIII

WELCOME TO THE SOUTHWEST

The year 1984 posed many unknowns at the time, but also things I had a yearning for since I was able to read about the southwest. I remember reading a quote that "Education is actually the pursuit of knowledge and knowledge can come from a walk in the desert. It does not have to come from flipping pages in a book. It is not harmful to explore a little bit of schooling, but don't buy into the idea that all what you are being taught is correct". I ponder those words as I travel through life and come to realize that teachers are only human and humans can and do error. But living amongst the cactus just had to be the greatest place in the world to be. I thought, maybe I would become a cowboy in my younger years. I had been to Arizona twice before and knew it was a place where I could spend a major amount of time.

In late winter of 1984 three of us guys from work and our spouses at the time took a weekend trip to Las Vegas. From there four of us rented a car and drove to Lake Havasu City in Arizona to visit Frank's parents who spent the winter there to get away from the cold winters in Wisconsin. Well, I had known about a manufacturing facility there and made pre-arrangements to stop in and discuss their business and my interest.

Several months later, I came home from work and my son Brian informed me a Human Resource lady called from Arizona and wanted to talk to me. I called back that same day, or was it even before he was done telling me, and accepted an interview the following week. Knowing how interested I was in their city and company along with my qualifications, they offered me an industrial engineering position the day after I returned home. I gladly accepted after hearing all the details.

We both gave our notice at work and said goodbye. It was almost like winning the lottery except we needed to spend two more weeks on our existing jobs. It took approximately three weeks to set all things in motion getting the house ready for sale and auctioning off the snow shovels. The personals were shipped via a moving company and we traveled by auto as a 5 day family vacation. The temps were around 115 degrees. I remember the song on the radio in the car as we drove into Lake Havasu City, *"The Heat Is On"* by Glenn Frey. I adjusted quite well and I think the rest of the family did also. After a few weeks of getting to know new friends in town and at work, it was time to get to know the area also. I was informed of a cousin named Leo (who was several years older) living in town. His younger sister Carol was in my class in high school. I got his phone number and gave him a call. We met at the San Francisco Bar and Grill on McCulloch Boulevard. We never met each other before so I looked for someone that looked like a brother to Carol. From that time on, we have always been doing things together and we spent a lot of time on the lake with his pontoon boat. Sunday morning the bars didn't open until 11:00 am in Arizona so we both being early risers just took the boat over to the other side of the lake to California and had our Bloody Mary. He was a merchant marine so was out to sea 4 months at a time and home for 2 months.

Later on as I got to know several people in town, I enrolled in a backpacking/hiking class at the community college in town. This gave me the opportunity to explore some canyons and mountains in Arizona with people of similar interests. For starters, the class took a terrific over night hike of 2 miles to some hot springs a few miles south of the Hoover Dam near the Colorado River. Water temperature was a constant 102 degrees with an area of approximately 30 square feet to soothe the tired feet. This wasn't bad for February in comparison to the Wisconsin winters. We had several other two day hikes on weekends before the big one.

With several more months of preparation and physical training, the class was ready to tackle the Grand Canyon. We camped out on the south rim on Friday night and woke up early Saturday morning to shake the snow off the tent and start our much anticipated hike down *Bright Angel Trail* to the canyon bottom. About half way down I had something coiled up in the middle of the trail. Rather than go around the rattlesnake, I waited patiently until he slithered to the side of the trail for protection from me. About two more miles from the Colorado River on the bottom the National Park has a small lodge with restaurant and some bunk houses called *Phantom Ranch*. This place is very much in demand for hikers to chow down breakfast, lunch or dinner. The prices are moderate and you need reservations, but it sure is healthier for the body than carrying that much extra food down. The park service also has several mule trains that make one trip a day to that point and the riders usually stay over night in the cabins. As hikers, we economized and carried our tents. Twelve miles down one day and then back up the same trail the next. Many rest stops were needed the next day on the way back to the top. Approximately 4 miles from the top at one of these stops a person (not part of our group) heard a thunder like sound, turned and ran because a boulder the size of a Volkswagen was loosened by the spring thaw and came tumbling down toward her. She didn't have time to grab her backpack. The boulder went right over the area where she was sitting. Lucky there was another boulder she had her backpack leaning against which caused the rolling boulder to bounce over it not causing any damage to the pack. The adventures of hiking that a photo can not capture.

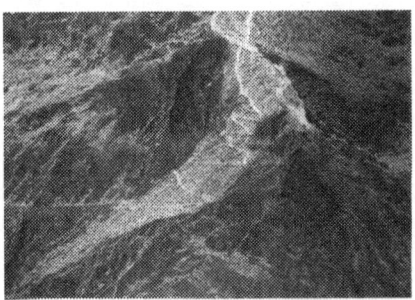

Bright Angel Trail

Of course, I did have some aches and pains at work on Monday. That was a total of 24 miles in two days carrying a 40 pound backpack with an elevation change of over 5,200 feet. It is not easier going down than up the canyon as one might think. You only get sore muscles in different areas of the legs, but the beauty you see down on the bottom makes it worth the pain.

Another attraction nearby was Laughlin, Nevada which had casinos and plenty of other live entertainment. It was located 70 miles upriver from LHC and close to half a dozen free tour busses to take you there for 6 hours and then back. At that time there were only six casinos and no stop lights in town. Now a bridge spans the Colorado River and at least ten stop lights to direct the increasing traffic for the added four casinos.

Meanwhile my position at McCulloch required almost bi-monthly trips to our Mexico operation in Juarez, Chihuahua. These were generally 2 week assignments with a commute from the company apartments in El Paso, Texas. Every trip was an adventure and an education. Time on weekends was spent exploring the surrounding area. Nights were usually early to bed and early to rise except when Friday and Saturday came around. In November '85 on one of those trips my son, Brian left to enlist in the Air Force but I didn't get to see him off because of my work in Mexico. His basic training was in San Antonio, Texas and early '86 he was transferred to Nellis AFB in Las Vegas.

CHAPTER IX

IN NEED OF DIVERSIONS

When my spouse departed right after Christmas 1985, it was an emotional struggle to maintain a happy lifestyle for a few years. Activities were usually planned to keep my mind from memories of times gone by. A fun filled New Years Eve was spent in Laughlin overnight with some friends and continued New Years Day in Arizona walking the main street in Oatman commingling with the wild burros. But it was still the first time in many years that I spent alone and now I knew how lonely it can be even with friends. I forced me to get out of the house and abandon the unwanted memories. One such venture took me, with a co-worker down to Parker, Arizona and a drive of seven miles off road in the desert to a so-called oasis which was named the *Desert Bar*.

Desert Bar

Because this was 4-wheel country, we had to take a truck to navigate the terrain. This person set up a little saloon on his acreage. It only had three sides to the building of about 6 feet deep by 10 feet wide and only 4 shabby bar stools and a couple stumps surrounding the place. No water or electricity and his hours were Friday, Saturday and Sunday till sundown because he had to bring in the supplies. Of course, the load was lighter on the way back for him. It made you scratch your head as to what he was trying to accomplish out in the middle of nowhere. To this day he is still open for business with numerous improvements with an eatery to satisfy your hunger.

After the sale of my dome house in Wisconsin April 1986, I purchased a new 2 bedroom 2 bath condo in central LHC. This I would call home again, temporarily. There were only eight units at Agave Bay so we all got to know each other quite well. Ken and Liz from across the driveway were retired school teachers from Phoenix. They had a second getaway home in LHC. They owned an airplane to commute to and from Phoenix and kept a truck and boat in LHC.

I had many flights to Laughlin with Ken and also fishing adventures on the lake. Ken taught me a lot about flying and I believe I could have gone solo. The two of us more or less took on the responsibility of maintaining the 8 unit complex to sustain reasonable association dues. Maintaining the inside of my condo, I only confirmed to myself that I did not have MGDB (Male Genetic Dirt Blindness). When you know that no one is going to clean up after you, a person learns to make cleanliness part of your life not that I ever had a problem with this task. I guess this is something that was instilled in me from my younger years.

As spring was leading us into summer, another co-worker and I with a couple friends drove to Long Beach, CA for a weekend trip. We took a boat over to Catalina Island to spend the night. The island was a 2nd home to the Wrigley family from Chicago. William Wrigley Jr. was instrumental in the development of the island and has a memorial dedicated to the family. Walking was the main mode of transportation on this island and our time was limited to do any earnest hiking. This was my first experience seeing the Pacific Ocean. I found it to be very alluring.

When returning home it was time to start making plans for another strenuous hike. This was a 3 day hike to another part of the Grand Canyon on the Havasupai Reservation. My youngest sister Nancy was one companion along with another co-worker. He introduced his 10 year old son to this adventure. Nancy was a sister I never did get to know as she was growing up because I moved out by the time she was two years of age. It was also a bonding experience.

The trip entailed some of the most wondrous sites in the southwest like Havasu Falls and Mooney Falls. On the second night of camping, we were startled by some wild horses trotting by within ten feet of our sleeping bags. Maybe we shouldn't have been there in the first place. It was somewhat difficult getting back to sleep after that awakening.

Later, in mid-summer, another co-worker and hiking buddy, Rex and I were scheduled for another trip to Mexico. This turned out to be one of several over the next few months. We had many common interests with which to utilize our spare time, like visiting Carlsbad Caverns in southeastern New Mexico. His life was pretty much distressed like mine and together we knew how to get matters back on track as some people at the 'Dallas Night Club' in El Paso would probably tell you.

My time now was spent driving to Las Vegas once a month because Brian was stationed there at Nellis AFB. It was a good get-a-way and there were always new casinos to explore. My cousin, Mike had a daughter and friend from Chilton stationed at Nellis also, so it was always a fun visit. These were the times when Las Vegas was less than a half million people which made it easy to drive around town and find excitement.

October was another two day hiking trip in the Sycamore Canyon Wilderness along the Verde River near Sedona, Arizona. This group included Rex, his friend Joyce and several other members of the hiking club. I was always wandering off on my own after camp was setup to explore areas not seen by the rest of the group. Off the trail about 100 feet I noticed a cave I had to investigate. Upon arriving at the entrance, I was greeted by a person living there and was invited inside. I was really hesitant because of his looks and his voice. Well, I went inside anyhow but always kept the doorway between him and myself. He informed he had a divorce that he never recovered from so decided to become a hermit out in the wild. I could easily see he had been living there for quite some time, possibly a year or more. Enough of that, so I left and wandered back to our campsite for more friendly confines.

When it came time for Thanksgiving in '86, I flew over to Oakland to spend some time with Larry in Alameda, California. The holiday weekend was spent touring the Bay area and doing whatever was of interest. That Christmas I flew back to Wisconsin unannounced to surprise the family. On Christmas Eve walking down the concourse in Green Bay I was met by my cousin Mike. His wife, Shirley saw me and let out a shrill and said, 'what are you doing here'. He was informed only to pick up a special delivery package and take it to my mom and dad's house. What a pleasant surprise for them when we pulled into the driveway that evening. It was probably the highlight of the year for me! Also plans were made at that time to have my brother-in-law Bob, who was terminally ill, to come out to Arizona for 3 weeks in February to get out of the cold temps in Wisconsin.

CHAPTER X

RAFTING THE COLORADO RIVER

When February came, Bob immediately jumped at the opportunity and rode out to Lake Havasu City with my sister Eunice and mom and dad. Bob enjoyed himself as much as he could even though he was losing ground to Hodgkin's disease. Bob went back to Wisconsin after several weeks to enjoy the winter. When Leo went back to sea, his friend Chu Hi from Korea and I attended a Patti Page concert at Riverside Resort which was quite a delight. We had a table right near the stage and Patti kept noticing that Korean lady particularly enjoying her entertainment. So when the concert was over Patti came to our table and sat down to chat with us for about five minutes. She told us her entertainment was very popular in South Korea during her world tours. Other concerts which I found interesting to attend at that resort at various times included; Sha Na Na, Tammy Wynette, Mel Tillis, Blood Sweat & Tears, Three Dog Night and The Mamas and The Papas just to name a few.

A much awaited whitewater raft trip we scheduled for June with my friends Rex and Joyce was soon upon us. A bus took us from Flagstaff where the car was parked, to an area just below the Glen Canyon Dam where we were met by a professional rafting company. We had three days of white-water and camping out under the stars each night as we splashed through the Grand Canyon for 80 miles. We elected to take the 3 day trip as opposed to taking the full river trip of 280 miles mainly because of cost. When we reached our destination near Phantom Ranch, it was rest time before the long hike out of the canyon on Bright Angel Trail once again. This time without a 40 pound backpack and only a small daypack with water, toothbrush and the usual camera of course. The raft trip continued from Phantom Ranch with a fresh group of candidates who had hiked down from the rim. That group enjoyed the remaining 200 miles of river in the beautiful Grand Canyon over the next 8 days.

It was only a couple weeks until the 4th of July when I flew over to Anaheim to meet Brian for a Brewer/Angel baseball game. It must have been a lackluster game because I don't remember who won. Besides Anaheim Stadium, it was a nice 3 day weekend taking in sites in Los Angeles. Another short notice trip was taken with cousin Leo and wife to LA again and a stop in Palm Springs before returning to LHC. These weekend getaways always had to coincide with my work scheduled trips to Mexico so planning more than a week ahead was almost impossible. At Christmas time I made another trip to visit family in Wisconsin even though it was cold, but being with family always compensated for that.

CHAPTER XI

TUCSON TRANSITION

By March of '88 it was time again for mom and dad to get out of the cold winter weather for a while. They stayed with me in Lake Havasu City for several weeks. A weekend trip took us over to Palm Springs where we attended a Milwaukee Brewers spring training baseball game. On our return we made a stop in Joshua National Monument to view the many Joshua trees.

During this point in time, my cousin Mike had a construction project on Roosevelt Lake north of Miami, Arizona. His company had a contract to build a bridge over that lake to eliminate the traffic going over the dam. It was a two year contract and gave me the opportunity to make several trips to that part of the state. When he didn't fly back to Wisconsin every two weeks his wife Shirley and son Brett would come to Arizona to stay with him for a week. Those times were usually spent with me either in Havasu area or Miami area and sometimes we were together even without Shirley.

To start out the summer, neighbor Helen and I took a weekend trip to tour the San Francisco Bay area. It was a place she never had the reason to visit so that was my excuse to go there and also visit my brother Larry to do some wine tasting in Napa Valley. By summers end, mom and dad had their 45th anniversary so I couldn't miss another trip back home to Wisconsin in September. Upon coming back home to work, I found I was scheduled for a three day business trip to Los Angeles to introduce a new electric chain saw to our corporate engineering department. As the headquarters were in close proximity to LAX airport, my stay was in Marina Del Rey right on the coast, therefore made the most of the three days with a fellow engineer from Havasu. We were also notified when we returned of our transfer date down to Tucson. Between then and year end, it was a hectic few months with working in Hermosillo and preparing my move to Tucson. Christmas this year was spent making that transition.

My transfer to Tucson offered many more opportunities in the southern part of Arizona that were otherwise beyond my getaway weekend reach. The area had lots of hiking, camping areas, convenience to a major airport and many trips to Mexico. I lived less than a mile from Sabino Canyon which is one of the more scenic places in southern Arizona.

Sabino Canyon

Taking a short break from unpacking, I looked through the information pages in the new phone book. This was before the days of internet. All a person had to do was dial certain 4 digit numbers and a recording would gave the information you were seeking. Well, I didn't check my lottery numbers yet. It was 4 days after the drawing so the recording announced the numbers. I picked the same numbers every week so some of them sounded familiar. I reached into my wallet and looked. I dialed the number again and sure enough, 5 out of 6 meant $575. And the one I missed was off by one digit. It would have been 5 million dollars. I always thought, mom was born one day too late because it was her birthday that was missed by one number. Oh well, again things happen for a reason. They are for your best interest determined by the Almighty. So, if you ever wonder why your prayers go unanswered, it is He who knows what is best for you now and for your future. This motivates me to pray for what I need, not for what I want.

Again, mom and dad spent a month with me in late winter to wait-out the arrival of spring in Wisconsin.

It was always good to have someone to show off the beauty and interesting sites of the southwest. One weekend we motored to Mexico and about 60 miles west of Hermosillo to an old fishing village. We stayed in Bahia de Kino which was somewhat upgraded for vacationers from the United States. It had a paved main road, but the older part of town which was known as Old Kino had no paved streets and potholes deep enough to hide a Volkswagen. Most residences in Old Kino were just a one room home and if you had two rooms you were rather well off in their standards. It was an exciting trip for all three of us. We stayed in a condo right on the Gulf of California.

April was time for some R&R so I took a trip to Europe to see my daughter Brenda who had been living there with a military friend. With my passport still in order from working in Mexico, I wanted to see some of Germany. Using a week's vacation and a little convincing at work, I got them to allow a couple extra days to visit the foreign division of our company in Italy. Upon landing in Frankfort and walking to the next gate of departure, I noticed something unusual. My wallet was missing from my back pocket with all my vacation spending money. That too gave me an important lesson and no one else was to blame. Never carry my wallet in the back pocket. Oh well. This trip continued on to Nuremburg where I spent a couple days with Brenda and also a place to borrow some money. My flight from there took me to northern Italy where I was met by a company rep at Milan airport. From Milan we drove north to the city of Lecco on Lake Como where I was provided with a nice 1st class hotel room for 2 nights. I was picked up in the morning and driven about 5 miles to the manufacturing facility in Valmadera. It was a great visit and had lunch in the employee cafeteria which I found to be very interesting. The first item in the chow line was a choice of a bottle of beer or wine but only one! The second evening I was treated to a small classy restaurant in Lecco located inside a cave like building. After the 3 hour feast of 7 courses and excessive wine, I was ready to crawl into bed. I don't know if the Italians are more impervious to these types of dinners or it was just me.

But my endeavors always seem to end too quickly for me to get tired of something. Italy was a place I could have spent a year or two. Anyhow, after my time there was over, I returned to Nuremburg to spend more time with Brenda. Most of my time was sightseeing in the east side of Germany with a quick trip to Munich with Brenda and her friend on the autobahn at over 100 mph. As for accidents, if your vehicle is not in A1 condition, you are not allowed on the autobahn. And if there is an accident, I don't know if they even bother investigating because they would never find all the pieces. Though the airports were heavily guarded, it was common to see 10 year old youngsters ride the subways alone. Going to places of interest included the little village of Rollhofen north of Nuremburg where my great-great-grandfather Ulrich Woelfel was born and raised in the mid 1800s before immigrating to America. The house was rebuilt but I did get a chance to talk with the present inhabitants who were very pleasant. After my goodbyes in Germany, my return flight back had a stop in New York and St. Louis before finally arriving back in Tucson.

Two weeks after getting back I was asked by my friends Rex and Joyce to join them on a drive down to Puerto Penasco in Sonora, Mexico. As if I needed another get-a-way weekend, but they didn't have to ask twice. This was a place of interest I always heard about and now we had the chance to see this tourist spot on the Sea of Cortez or as some would refer to as the Gulf of California. Lots of fresh shrimp and tequila to keep us entertained which was just 60 miles below the Arizona border through Organ Pipe National Monument.

In June I was enlisted to help with the shut down of our Juarez, Mexico operation which was now combined with the Hermosillo operation. It was a sad occasion to see those people out of work but life goes on.

The end of July it was time for my 25th Class reunion so that obligated another trip back home to Wisconsin again. Now I needed to start accruing some more vacation time, so I thought.

Summer was over quickly and then September came. With a little foresight, a person should have seen what was going on, but when work activities occupy most of your time, we don't see what is happening around us. It was then, one half the engineering staff was informed, the company was forced to make a rather large cutback and I happened to be included. I wasn't even done studying that area of the country yet. Even though we were given a trivial severance package, they did enlist a company to assist us with finding new employment. They were in the business to assist displaced workers with a weekly program and they were paid for by your previous employer. That weekly session was very beneficial in generating interest from other companies but it took almost four months to land a new position. Now I had a temporary renter with me in my apartment. With me out of work, Tom and I took every chance we had to check out places I didn't see yet. Tom was a tool room supervisor and my close friend with McCulloch so we had a lot of common interest. He wanted to experience old Mexico as a family so I drove him, wife Judy and son Stephen down into Mexico as far as Hermosillo with their car and then spent the night in town with them. The next day they continued on to Bahia de Kino area while trying to cure their upset stomachs. Meanwhile I flew back to Tucson.

For Thanksgiving, my brother Larry flew down from Calistoga and Brian drove from Las Vegas to Tucson so the three of us could spend a delightful time in Puerto Penasco to have our Thanksgiving dinner. This pleasant drive resulted in our grilling fresh shrimp right off the shrimp boats for dinner on the beach. We had plenty of Tecate for relaxation and just walking around the shrimp seaport to pass the time.

Later in December, I had an interview in Shreveport, Louisiana with a competitor of McCulloch which I almost accepted. Except I wanted to stay in the Southwest so I stalled for a week to follow-up on another possibility. During this same period I had been up to the Navajo Reservation to interview at an OEM electronics assembly operation started up by General

Motors Corporation. They made me an offer which I accepted because it was still in Arizona and a beautiful part at that being in the Painted Desert. Unfortunately this move also necessitated me to live in the mountains of Arizona with snow in winter.

As a farewell with Rex and Joyce, we attended a Stevie Nicks concert at TCC arena in Tucson. This goodbye was only temporary because we had plenty of good times together and I knew there would be more. Now we would have 300 miles between us though.

On a relocation trip to Flagstaff in December, I located a suitable apartment on the east side. This made the commute slightly shorter because I didn't have to drive through town. Upon returning to Tucson, I soon left for the holidays to be with family in Wisconsin with a stop in Minneapolis. We exchanged some passengers and de-iced the plane before continuing on to Milwaukee.

CHAPTER XII

BACK TO SNOW COUNTRY

When I returned back to Tucson the first week of January in 1990, it was now time to head up to Flagstaff to start life in the high country, which being a college town gave me plenty action. My commute was 100 miles round trip to Leupp every day with a change in elevation from 7,200 feet in Flagstaff to around 4,200 feet in Leupp. In winter it was snowing in town while at work it was sunny and warm. Many days we would get out of work with a sunny sky and then look toward the mountains and see nothing but white which meant we had to drive into a snow storm. There were several other engineers from town. We always looked out for one another. After several months in the area, I joined a singles group to maybe meet some friends that enjoyed the outdoors like me. It didn't take long and I became interested in this one girl that seemed to fit that profile. Julie was kind of a perpetual student at Northern Arizona University with various types of employment to maintain her lifestyle. We took many hikes, sometimes with other companions but mostly by ourselves. Several of them took us into the Grand Canyon. Those hikes into the canyon were always appealing to me.

March came and because I was always getting positive information on Radial Keratotomy from several previous patients, I decided to attend a presentation on that procedure. It was enough to convince me I was a good candidate. My right eye was done March 2nd and one week later my left eye. I could notice immediately when driving home, there was improvement and have never regretted since. Now I can rollover in bed and see the numbers on the alarm clock without probing for my glasses on the night stand in the morning. To try out my new sight, I took a rail trip on the Grand Canyon Railroad with mom, dad, Larry, Bob and Eunice. This was an old steam locomotive that went from Williams to the Grand Canyon and back. This was an adventure we all enjoyed though we were held up by some faux cowboys on the way back to Williams. We all got away without losing any valuables, but we had a good laugh. In June, I took my usual trip back to Wisconsin to visit family.

That summer I had several weekend trips with Julie, one of which was to Los Alamos, New Mexico to visit her sister Cecelia. She was employed at Los Alamos National Laboratory during her time off at the University of Arizona. She majored in nuclear engineering at school in Tucson and worked at that laboratory during the summer. A drive over to Santa

Fe ten miles away was a good chance to tour the state capital and all the other touristy type things.

Working with the Navajo people in Leupp was a wonderful educational experience and one that I will value the rest of my life. More people should have the opportunity to work with Native Americans and experience the cultures that most don't understand.

For the Thanksgiving holiday weekend, Julie and I took a drive up to Utah to hike Bryce and Zion National Parks. Because of overnight cold temps, there was no overnight hiking this time and nights were spent in a Best Western.

Just before the Christmas holiday season it got down to 20 below zero in the mountains one night. With the plant shut down for the holidays, we packed our suitcases and headed down to Sonora, Mexico. It was cold there also at 50 degrees but much warmer than Flagstaff. I had several past associates from work at McCulloch to visit down there. We wanted to experience Christmas in an old fishing town in Mexico called Bahia de Kino. I will always cherish how much they enjoy the season without all the commercialism that we get hung up on in this country. We call it development. I attended a Christmas Day service at their church that was quite an occasion also. No pews but benches to sit on. Some people brought their dogs along that would lay down in the aisle beside them. I believe I was the only gringo in attendance. On Christmas day we met the Chris Garcia family. We drove around town looking to buy some fresh fish for our dinner. We stopped in this shabby saloon and asked. A gentleman offered some information in broken English. Chris invited us to his house down the street to spend some time until the fish supplier was available. Chris could speak some English and Julie was proficient in Spanish so we managed quite well. Later that afternoon their 12 year old friend Monica the babysitter for their kids came for a visit. When we discovered her birthday was in 2 days, we drove around this village to find someone that would make a birthday cake for us. After several hours of searching, we found a lady that was eager to that task. We picked up the cake the next day and delivered it to the Garcia house. The birthday girl was there also and we presented her with the very first birthday cake in her 13 years. She was overwhelmed and her smile went from ear to ear. That instance had just as big of an impact on us. Our tears were fought back to see her joy. It was truly an enjoyable Christmas I will never forget.

Now back to the cold winter and snow in Flagstaff. A lot can be said about the reason why I moved to the southwest. But I made the best of the situation for the interim. Many trips were made down the mountain to Sedona which was 20 degrees warmer and usually sunny. Hiking was a favorite pastime while visiting the fantastic Red Rock vistas. Between local sightseeing and hiking, usually that was enough to keep my mind off the cold winter. In March, mom and dad made their annual trip out west but this time they had to put up with winter in the high country. I remember dad saying after he shoveled the 11" snow fall from the sidewalk, "if I wanted to shovel snow, I would have stayed home in Wisconsin". Well, the following weekend we took a quick trip down to Tucson to visit friends and savor the warm country. With the weekend trips to warmer climes like Sedona, Montezuma Castle and Verde River Canyon rail trip, the twosome managed okay. After a couple weeks of winter, the two were sent to LHC to enjoy themselves in a more pleasant climate before they returned home. In April when winter was losing ground and spring was coming alive with wild flowers, the outdoors were getting more attractive again for hiking. Several hikes into the Grand Canyon with friends were enough for the time being.

In spring a trip was taken to New York with two business associates to evaluate a new product the company was considering. It was only a two day trip but we crammed hours of sightseeing both days, besides doing what we were there for. We stayed in Yonkers and toured much of Manhattan.

June was time for another compulsory visit with family in Wisconsin. That trip included a side trip to Door County and to Washington Island with a stay overnight at a Gills Rock Bed & Breakfast. I usually stretched my vacation over holidays to make it last longer without needing an abundance of accrued vacation time at my workplace. By Monday after the 4th of July, I was back at my job. Before September arrived, Brenda made a surprise appearance from Germany. We took in the sites surrounding Flagstaff, including the canyon. After she left to go back to Germany, several hikes were back in order. Julie and I hiked Petrified Forest National Park one weekend and a week later in the Hualapai Mountains near Kingman. I also got to know and make very good friends with Ron and Kerri George family since I carpooled with him to

Leupp everyday. He is also an outdoor enthusiast like me with a lot in common. We usually carpooled to the pool hall once a week also and had several camping trips in our times together. They are very dear friends and to this day we still have our good times.

As the summer closed out, Julie and I were inspired by this wonderful and secluded hideaway for our so called unification. Why, I don't know because things were endurable just the way they were. Anyhow it was a nice get-together for the family and friends that could make it. Our honeymoon took us on a trip to Hawaii and we stayed at a B&B overlooking a 1000 foot waterfall. That trip also convinced me of another wonderful place to explore. So when we returned home, discussions led to a move to Hawaii. Just pull up stakes and go someplace warm, as life was short and we only go around once.

Before I could leave Flagstaff though, I would complete a class taken at work called "Cultural Awareness" taught by the school district administrator. He was non Navajo professor enlisted in the education of our Native Americans. He lived on the edge of the reservation. He and his wife had a residence in a remote area near the reservation. He managed with self produced utilities most people take for granted like phone, electricity and cable TV. When our six week class was complete, he invited all participants out to his house for a cookout. He had a Navajo lady do the preparation of the mutton and we did all the eating. This entire experience was to educate us Caucasian employees about the Navajo culture and aid us in working with the people. We had approximately

12 people from Flagstaff that managed the Navajo workforce. Usually 5 or 6 of them were here from General Motors in Ohio on a temporary assignment and the remainder being locals like myself.

So in October, I drove out to Leupp for my last day October 31, 1991 at Tooh Dineh Industries. We stayed in a motel in Flagstaff the night before departure because we already vacated our apartment. It was snowing quite heavy that morning, but still made a stop for breakfast at Ms Zip's cafe with Julie. Got to Leupp about 7 am but didn't get too much accomplished because of all the good-byes. Left work at 11:30 am to head back to Flagstaff. They had received over 10 inches of snow by then. We put our luggage in the car and headed for Las Vegas where we stayed at the Boardwalk Casino that night. The next day we headed up to Reno by way of Death Valley and Scotty's Castle. We spent our first night in Beatty, Nevada at hole in the wall motel. We left early in the morning for California. Fortunately there was no snow to go through at around 10,000 foot elevation up in Donner's Pass. We made a quick stop in Fairfield to visit my cousin Leo who had relocated there from LHC. Making our way up Napa Valley, we were greeted by my brother Larry in Calistoga by late that afternoon. After a couple days in Calistoga with Larry, we headed down to Oakland to ship the car to Hawaii and then spent the last night in San Francisco. It was by coincidence rather than planning that my son Brian and wife Suk had just flown in from 2 years over in Korea. A wonderful night was had by all before our departure the next morning for Maui. It was unfortunate more time couldn't be spent together because it was 2 years since we had last seen each other. He was on the way to his reassignment at Eglin AFB near Fort Walton Beach, Florida. It was several more years before we would see each other again.

CHAPTER XIII

ISLAND LIFE

Julie and I arrived on Maui the first week in November of 1991. After one night at the Banana Bungalow we decided we needed something a little more upscale. Well, it was dark when we arrived so how was I to know? It didn't have windows and with eerie noises outside all night, we were ready to leave in the morning. It must have been a hangout for local people in Wailuku that didn't have anywhere else to stay. The next day as we were touring the town on foot we stopped at a bank to open an account and got on the subject of a rental available. Well this lady just happened to know of a place in Haiku that was available immediately. We took a drive to inspect and immediately signed the papers. This was a small 2 story, 2 bedroom house built on to the landlord residence that served our needs just right. Later that month on my birthday we took a sunset sail for my first experience on the waters of the South Pacific islands. It wasn't long and Julie found employment a mile away just in time to get us invited to their Christmas Party.

For pastime, I did get a chance to attend the PGA Senior Skins golf tournament in Kaanapali which was on the northwest side of Maui. Was great to watch pros like Lee Trevino and Gary Stockton up close and live. I always wondered why the official held up those little signs that read QUIET just as the player prepared to address the ball, as some hecklers were chastised. Why, I don't know. Any other sport the spectators get to rouse the concentration of athletes.

During my employment dry spell, I had the pleasure to meet Tony and Lucy. They were our neighbors from about 5 acres away and were island natives in their mid 70s. An operation on his eye in San Francisco required their only trip to the mainland during their 70 plus years. Lucy was the farmer type and maintained a huge yard keeping it from being invaded with undesirable vegetation. Many fruit trees, grape wines, avocado, banana, macadamia, mango and papaya trees kept her busy during daylight hours. Their two steers usually kept the pasture grass (remnants of sugar cane field) from getting too tall. The steers were also supplemented with high protein grain to enhance the beef for slaughter. Well, anyhow, they were always replaced by 2 young calves and no matter what their color, they were always named Blackie. Tony was a retired county forestry worker who was totally blind since one year after his retirement. He lost his left eye during an accident at work and his right eye was lost when he had a stroke one year after he retired. Most people would probably be despondent in his condition, but not good old Tony. He was very interesting and he just enjoyed someone to "talk story" with, as they say in Hawaii. We shared many stories about our childhood, even though we were from two different generations. Many took us well into the night and I would end up walking home in the dark. Our first Thanksgiving dinner on Maui was with Tony and Lucy. I guess Lucy she saw the effect I had on Tony's disposition. I was his buddy while she maintained her multitude of flower beds.

Our weekends or rather Julie's days off were usually spent exploring the island. In December, I accepted an interview over on the Big Island with Mauna Loa Macadamia Nut Corporation which I was anxiously waiting for. Within a few days I was offered a position as Packaging Manager with them and relocated to Hilo right after Christmas. Christmas was spent with Tony and Lucy and at that time they were informed of our relocation to the Big Island. They were happy for the job opportunity and sad we were leaving Maui, but I informed them we would be back often to visit.

A couple days after Christmas, I received word from my friends in Tucson that my very dear friend Tom had passed away. I had spoken to him less than two weeks before when he was in the hospital fighting his cancer.

With relocation over to the Big Island, temporary lodging was provided in some nice villas for several weeks until a more permanent house was located in Hilo. This is the island where we honeymooned and I was impressed already at that time. So what if it rained

130 inches a year, it was a warm rain! This island provided lots of hiking and with an active volcano always creating new areas for evaluation. It was a place that would generate much leisure activity. At the weekly Farmers Market in downtown Hilo, I met an elderly gentleman named Jakob from Switzerland who was attending the university in Hilo. Even though he was 74 years of age, his form of transportation was a bike loaned to him by some students. On weekends he would spend his days with us touring the island. One such occasion we had a barbeque in a picnic area right on the coast, grilling one of his favorite foods, a German bratwurst. On other weekends to get out of the rain, a trip to Kona on the sunny side of the island was usually my area of excitement.

In June, we had our first visitors from the mainland. Larry and Doreen came to experience life in the islands and were given a first hand guided tour around the Big Island for several days. Spring and summer weekends were always used exploring National Parks and Monuments as well as State Parks. Besides Volcanoes National Park and several other National parks, a State Park of special interest was Lava Tree State park where the area was overrun with lava years ago and all the live trees were smothered with lava to around ten feet up the trunk. Because the trees were full of sap, the lava was cooled surrounding the trunk while lava in the surrounding area subsided leaving stumps of 10 feet high. The trees eventually died off leaving a shell of hard lava with an empty center when the stump decayed.

Lava Tree State Park

Another adventure took us picking wild bananas on land once used for growing sugar cane owned by the parent company of Mauna Loa. These little secret spots that bananas grew were located through a friend recently retired from the sugar plantation.

Deep sea fishing with some friends on a private boat had me thinking that I was going to be the next Gilligan. Approximately 6 miles out of Hilo, the engine gave out on his 38 foot fishing boat which resulted in several SOS pleas with no response. In the meantime, the boat owner was frantically trying to find the problem with no success. It wouldn't have been so serious but we didn't have any fish for our first meal lost at sea. After several hours, a Japanese fisherman picked up on our distress call and came to our rescue. He towed us back to Hilo harbor late afternoon before the skipper had to assign our places to sleep that night for the six of us. Following that exciting episode, a month later I had the opportunity to go fishing again with one of the suppliers we had at work. This time it was out of Kona and with a charter fishing boat that was kept in better condition. We did catch some little

10 pound fish which we used for bait but still no luck with marlin.

On the Fourth of July weekend, we took a trip over to Kauai to see how other islanders existed. It was a smaller island and was home to a subsidiary of Mauna Loa in the business of producing guava puree from their 4,000 acre guava orchard. Less than six weeks after we returned, hurricane Iniki devastated the island of Kauai. This storm left little undamaged. It would take years to rebuild. Some like Coco Palms Resort (setting for "Blue Hawaii" film) were never restored. The building is still standing but no longer open to the public. I read the sale of the now vacant building is being held up in litigation because the firm owning it was located in the World Trade Center building.

It was barely a year when Julie decided she had enough of island life, severed ties and returned to the mainland. Again, life goes on. I had several family visitors from the mainland to help overcome my somewhat dismal times. In the meantime Judy, the widow of my departed friend Tom, relocated to the Big Island from Tucson.

In fall of my first year at work I heard a new lava flow was moving toward the site Julie and I picnicked. Within 2 days the area would be inundated with fresh lava. This created much excitement at work for me. That evening as the lava approached the picnic site, Judy and I drove down to the coast to get a closer look. We parked on the side of the highway and walked about a mile to experience the approaching flow as it entered the ocean. As we watched the spectacle, we were soon approached by several park rangers. They advised us it would be in our best interest to leave area immediately because the lava was about to cross the highway between us and where the cars were parked. After a few minutes we decided it was time to go. Sure enough, news the next morning stated the picnic area was no longer available and was completely covered with the new flow.

Every couple months I flew over to Maui to visit my friends Tony and Lucy. There were always some things that needed attention in the yard. Also, parts of the island that I didn't see when I lived there needed discovery. In December I took a trip to Las Vegas to meet mom, dad, my brother Larry, his friend Doreen and my friend Ron George from Flagstaff. Dad needed to take a test drive with their new car from Wisconsin. Mom and dad needed some time away from home before winter really settled in. It was only a 3 day weekend into which we crowded a week of activity. When I returned to Hawaii I upgraded myself with a new computer system from Radio Shack. This was probably the eve of the Internet. I needed travel data close at hand rather than making frequent trips to the library.

New Year's holiday weekend was spent in Kona to enjoy some sunshine and also spend New Year's Day deep sea fishing. We had no luck for marlin. It was an unusually cold drizzly day to spend on the 8 foot high seas. Anyhow, the harbor was a welcome sight at day's end.

By mid March of '93 I had some much welcomed guests from Wisconsin stay with me for several weeks. It was the year of mom and dad's 50th wedding anniversary and they needed some pictures of Hawaii.

50th anniversary pose on Maui

A couple weeks later my daughter Brenda made a visit from Germany to decide if island life was what she yearned for. Mom and dad never did have a dull moment while in Hawaii and never did stop moving. They got to know my neighbors quite well. A few trips were made to view the volcano as it was always emitting fresh lava flows at that time. My dad and I had the experience to poke a stick into the advancing 2,000 degree lava as it slowly came toward us. Mom had kept her distance as methane gas from green vegetation being covered with this hot lava caused periodic explosions in the area.

We also flew over to Maui for a weekend to visit my friends Tony and Lucy. After returning, it was almost time for my folks to go back home because winter was about over in Wisconsin. I had pre-arranged to fly back to San Francisco with them to attend another brothers wedding. A stopover night was spent in Honolulu to visit Pearl Harbor Memorial and just rest up before the wedding. The aircraft we had originated from Tokyo.

It was that airline policy to serve complimentary cocktails for the duration of the international flight. With assigned seats next to the galley we never had an empty glass for long. It did make for a very short flight though. We were met at the airport by my brother Jim from Michigan and a sister Nancy from Colorado. They didn't want to know us when we got off the plane. Larry and Doreen's wedding ceremony took place in St. Helena and the reception followed in Calastoga. By Sunday I was on my way back to Hilo after a month of special company.

July brought my hiking partners, Rex and Joyce from Tucson to Hilo for a 10 day visit. That meant more fun miles on the feet as we hiked to places I wouldn't go alone. Toward the end of summer, it was time for me to take a week for the 50th anniversary in Wisconsin plus an extra week for a workshop in Madison. That workshop just happened to coincide with the scheduled trip for the anniversary. Prior to that week in Madison, I took the pleasure of a two day trip to Door County and car ferry over to Washington Island. Upon returning back to Gills Rock we had to enjoy their famous Norwegian fish boil that is so popular in that area. The night was spent at a bed & breakfast. These visits to Wisconsin were always topped off with several mouth-watering steak dinners at our favorite Schwarz's Supper Club in St. Anna.

My cousin Leo came to Hilo in September with Matson's sugar barge from Crockett, California to load up with sugar from all the plantations in Hawaii. Being a merchant marine, this was a trip he made periodically. Usually it was an opportunity to see one another even though the stop was only for one day. November my older brother Jim, who was in a similar solitary situation as I, came out from Michigan to spend the Thanksgiving holidays. We made the most of our allotted time with a weekend side trip over to Maui to again meet my friends Tony and Lucy. While Jim was visiting me in Hilo, we also experienced a little shower of 12 inches in a 24 hour period. This wasn't normal rainfall even though there were much heavier rains at times. Usually the next day there is very little sign of such a torrential rain.

My position required me to work very closely with suppliers on the mainland and also a few in the islands. This involved flying over to Honolulu for meetings with our marketing department. The mainland suppliers would make a visit to Hilo approximately every two months as a good will trip, but in December I was invited over to Seattle to visit our corrugated box supplier. This was a very informative trip not only to see how corrugated boxes were made, but to see the city of Seattle also. Highlights included the Space Needle and Pike Street Market and enjoying the seafood chowder of course. I was barely back to Hilo for a couple weeks when I flew to Tucson to see my friends Rex and Joyce. Hiking in the Tucson area and a drive down to Nogales, Mexico was our pastime.

I enjoyed my hiking activities in Volcanoes National Park mainly because it was a constant changing park. I made an effort to take in the park for some informative walks conducted by the rangers or with some friends almost weekly. Before my time in 1991 on the Big Island, a small village on the southeastern part of the island was overcome with lava. The coast line was extended out to sea by a hundred acres and all new land becomes part of the National Park system. This gave us an opportunity to plant new vegetation in this area which was encouraged by the park service. I gathered numerous coconuts as many other people did, from other rainforest on the island and transplanted them in the flow to start a new forest. Because the lava had broken down into a fine black sand by the surf action, digging holes by hand for the coconuts was easy. Apparently the new soil contained some nutrients to give the trees a chance to flourish.

During this time, our supplier from Seattle invited several of us from work on a helicopter tour of the volcano and surrounding area. This was an experience to just hover over the glowing vent of hot lava. We observed many waterfalls our way back from the one hour trip.

In February, I picked up two of my sisters, Eunice and Nancy at the airport. They came to evaluate my life style and have some fun in the process. More coconuts were planted and another trip to Maui to see Tony and Lucy. By now Brenda was living on Maui also. Two days before those two sisters left, another sister Ellen, husband Tom and daughter Katrina arrive for a week of guide service which was always to my fancy. Plentiful warm hugs were my gift from all. The group of six charted the deserted island. No wait, it wasn't deserted at all, but we did have adventures.

CHAPTER XIV

RETURN FROM ENCHANTMENT

April of 1994 it came time to move back to Arizona, though it was like being torn between two places. I flew into San Francisco and was met by my brother Larry. I stayed at his house for a week until my car was delivered to Oakland harbor. When it finally arrived, I drove to Lake Havasu City to do some serious job searching and spend some time with friends. Several weeks went by before I ended up back at my previous employer on the reservation. I now returned to the high country only because employment presented itself and finances were getting tight. My residence was found through some friends that knew of their previous place being available. This was a 3 story house with the lower level being a rental property which bordered on the Coconino National Forest. I felt my time there would be of short duration but ended up 18 months before I found something in a more acceptable climate. It had a two acre lot with wildlife like porcupines and deer to see which made it somewhat more bearable. The landlord always gave me responsibility for the harvest in their nice garden when they left for vacation. I did not mind that assignment. The Flagstaff area had plenty national monuments and parks to hike which kept me from going bananas.

A weekend in August, my dear friends, the George family, invited me along on a camping excursion to the Kaibab Plateau on the North Rim of the Grand Canyon. Twenty miles from civilization listening to the elk and coyotes at night was good for the fortitude. Later that month I also embarked on a rail trip with friends Judy and Stephen from Lake Havasu City. We went from Durango to Silverton Colorado along the Animas River through some of the most scenic mountains I have ever seen. Returning home, we went through Mesa Verde National Park home of some Indian ruins kept in near pristine condition even after 800 years.

This being the year for our 30th Class reunion enabled me to take another vacation to Wisconsin. I never missed one of the every five year events. Proceedings were held in Elkhart Lake at Barefoot Bay Resort in September. At conclusion of the party and because of walking distance to my sister Dori and Jim's house, I elected to spend the night with them.

Back at the homestead where I usually spend my vacation, work was being completed on the family mini golf course. Each one of Linus and RoseMary's nine children had the responsibility to design one hole.

Our designated hole was laid out in the form of the number where we ranked in family order with the final layout and obstacles personalized by the individual. So we had big concrete numbers covered with green outdoor carpeting. They were scattered on a half acre of vacant land near our farm pond at what we call the Woelfel Pond Resort. It was complete with a lodge, volleyball court, horseshoe pit, two acre pond and lots of lawn that needed mowing. Many of our family gatherings are held at this park-like setting.

Family golf course

On my return home to Flagstaff, it was getting to be fall color season with more adventure walks into the forest for photographing. Now I could see where all the photos in National Geographic were taken of the aspen leaves in their golden conclusion before coming to rest on the ground in preparation for winter. Though the forests were appealing, I could feel the chill in the air and knew the snow wasn't far behind. On occasional weekends I drove over to Laughlin, Nevada for encouragement to pull me through the winter. On a particular trip taken there for my birthday in November, I left Flagstaff with good roads for 30 miles until Williams. This was Interstate 40 and from there the snow started falling, but I thought in 20 miles, I would be in a lower elevation and it would be fine again. Well, the lower the elevation, the worse it got as I was only driving about 15 mph. It would have been foolish to turn back because then I would be driving with the storm instead of through it. By the time I got to the east side of Kingman, there was over 10 inches on the highway with only one lane open. Lots of vehicles in the ditch upside down and most were SUVs that thought they could handle any road conditions at normal high speeds. It was by far the worst driving conditions I ever experienced even in Wisconsin. What a relief when I was in Laughlin and no snow after a 5 hour trip which was usually under 3 hours. The trip back on Sunday was on good highway all the way.

At Christmas time a quick trip was made back to Wisconsin for with the family. No one except my sister Ellen and husband Tom knew about it. They picked me up at the airport in Milwaukee on Christmas day morning and drove up to the homestead to meet the rest of the family for dinner. The year went out with lots of warm hugs. Then I flew back to Las Vegas and drove to Flagstaff to begin the New Year.

February, I had my traditional much-welcomed visitors from Wisconsin. This always enabled me to take in some activities that I was not inclined to do at other times alone. After exhausting our list of activities in Flagstaff and surrounding area, (which are somewhat limited at that time of year for snowbirds) they continued on to LHC and Laughlin before heading back to Wisconsin. In June the landlord and family took a six week vacation to Spain. They introduced me to the house-sitter named Christine during the time they were gone. She was a school teacher from Lake Havasu City taking some college courses at Northern Arizona University for her Masters. After several weeks of shyness on both of our parts, we finally started talking and doing some outdoor activities together like hiking. We enjoyed taking in the abundance of national monuments and parks in Northeast Arizona and the Navajo Reservation.

Canyon De Chelly

When the homeowner arrived back from the trip, school was finished and she moved back to LHC, but we kept in touch and had many good times for several years.

Late in the summer of 1995 our family celebrated a 150 year reunion for my Great-great Grandfather. This event was for all his ancestors who immigrated to this country in 1845 from Germany. This occasion was in the planning stage for years and was finally becoming a reality. My brother Jim was working diligently on our genealogy over eight years and was in the final stages of putting together a book for this electrifying event.

An event of this magnitude was not to be missed by me. Relatives from all over the country and some from overseas were also making plans to attend. With all the greetings and celebrating taking place in New Holstein Civic Park, the total attendance was over 1,200 with many more relatives sending letters of regret for not being able to attend.

In November, after much discussion, a friend Bob and I took Amtrak Rail from Flagstaff to Los Angeles and then up to Oakland via the scenic Pacific Coast. Once in Oakland, we hitched a ride with my brother Larry to the airport in San Francisco for a ten day trip to Hawaii touring Maui to see Brenda and my friends on the Big Island. Most of the time while I was visiting my friends, Bob was exploring the volcano area. Bob was quite impressed with the beauty of the islands and I enjoyed showing him the challenge I had when living there. There was much more to see and do yet, but my time was limited and we needed to get back to the mainland. Again, we were met at the airport by Larry who took us to his house in Calistoga for a couple days. Thanksgiving eve we rode with them down to Fresno to have Thanksgiving dinner with some cousins we met at the big family reunion in August. Our turkey and ham was put in a three foot pit with hot coals buried by Bryce the night before. It was like a luau, only with a turkey. Was it ever scrumptious! This was an exciting experience as we lodged for two nights in an old seminary building under management by another cousin Father Rod. The weekend was outstanding as we reminisced about the recently held reunion in Wisconsin where they were all in attendance. The event drew to a close with hugs and goodbyes the last day. It was now time for Bob and me to catch Amtrak in Fresno back to Flagstaff.

During the Christmas holidays I left home in the high country to visit friends in Tucson and took a side trip to Nogales, Mexico. Sabino Canyon hikes as always, took the most important amount of our time together.

CHAPTER XV

TREASURES OF NORTHEAST ARIZONA

Once the holidays were over, I took every opportunity to squander the weekends in the warmer climes of Lake Havasu City or Laughlin. Christine was usually up to a nice trek in the desert with the Colorado River providing an abundance of trails to check out. I was still driving the Pontiac Lemans that I shipped over from Hawaii and it didn't like the terrain it had to go through so I got myself a Subaru Outback. This was all-wheel drive and had room in the back for sleeping on my many weekend excursions. Probably 10 per cent of the miles were off road. The only negative aspect was that it lacked the horsepower for some of the places it was forced to maneuver. One such off-road drive was to see Grand Falls which formed on the Little Colorado River on the Navajo Reservation. This place involved a drive of 10 miles on a dirt road lavished with pot holes. It was quite a scene after a rain to see the chocolate colored water cascade down several hundred feet as it continued on its way to the mighty big Colorado River. Usually by time it reached the big river, the chocolate colored mud and sand was filtered out and it became a nice turquoise blue as the two merged. Weekend trips were also taken again to several national monuments like Canyon De Chelly, Painted Desert and Petrified Forest in the Arizona northeast. Being in Flagstaff did have advantages. It made the distances much shorter to these treasures.

Monument Valley

July came and it was time to celebrate my sister Dori's 40th birthday at the homestead down by our meeting grounds at the pond resort in Wisconsin. She was glad to only have one 40th but a fun time was had by all regardless. When I arrived back in Flagstaff, I was informed by the landlord the house was sold and the new owners would take possession in six weeks. That was fine with me, but when they told me the rent would be double, I decided it would be in my best interest to relocate to a studio type apartment because

I didn't want to spend another winter there anyhow. Now I was forced to do some serious job hunting in the lower elevation. I accepted a supervisor position in Kingman where I managed long 14 hour days but never more than 3 days in succession. That was ok for several months but I was literally exhausted when I got home. I only had time for a quick bite to eat then off to bed so I could rise in time for work the next day.

A Saturday in November, I was at Riverside Resort viewing a preview video near the celebrity showroom when a person came up behind me and tapped me on the shoulder saying, "those are some pretty funny guys, aren't they". I turned and looked to see Dick Smothers standing beside me. We had a nice short chat and we both went on our way. That evening I did go to Tom and Dick's performance and was amused until my sides ached. I did get an opportunity for both of them to autograph my program after their show. Christmas was spent in Tucson with friends during the holiday company shutdown.

When the weather started to be more obliging, Christine and I longed for hiking in the Cerbat Mountains near Kingman. In those mountains there was an almost abandoned mining town called Chloride with maybe 100 residents left. In the nearby mountains were some unusual rock formations that were artistically painted by some artist from Las Vegas years ago. Those paintings were kind of modern day petroglyphs. Gradually, I could tell my body was starting to fatigue from the long hours at work. This became more obvious to me on hikes.

By this time, I had enough of those long hours so I forced myself to resign from that company. The money was good but it was wrecking my body. That was near the end of May, so in June when school was over, Christine and I took a trip over to Maui to again see Brenda and spend some time on the Big Island visiting my friends and of course take in some snorkeling.

After that trip, I took a drive back to Wisconsin for a family visit. All this time, the summer had me searching for gainful employment again. This trip also had me take a car ferry over to Michigan with mom, dad and a sister Nancy. It was 60 miles on Lake Michigan with calm seas the entire route docking in Ludington. From there we drove to Lansing to see my older brother Jim and then to do some sightseeing in the Upper Peninsula across the Mackinaw bridge. When my time was up in Wisconsin, I headed to Minnesota to pick up Christine who had been there visiting her family. On the way back home, it gave me the opportunity to visit some of the national parks I never had the chance to see. Now I had someone with me to share the sites. First we traveled to Mount Rushmore in South Dakota, then Bighorn National Forest, Yellowstone and the Grand Tetons in Wyoming. As we drove through Utah we took in Bryce National Canyon, Zion National Park, through Las Vegas then home to Kingman, Arizona. A couple weeks later in July, I drove to Las Vegas again to meet with my sister, Dori and family who were there on vacation. For me it was just a two day get-together and allowed some time to experience the town together.

By the middle of August, my job search was becoming more productive and I accepted a temporary position at General Motors. I am on my way to Michigan for this contract job at GM in Pontiac. Left Flagstaff at 7 a.m., arrived in Amarillo, Texas about 7 or 8 PM. The time includes getting stopped by a Texas Ranger as I was coming in to Amarillo at only 3 miles over the speed limit but because my car being fully loaded with my belongings, I looked suspicious. After he couldn't find what he was looking for, he issued a warning. All he could write was "I was exceeding the 70 mph speed limit". Well, that was enough driving and excitement for the day so I stayed there in town even after that encounter. After working for a couple weeks in Michigan, I flew back to Kingman for a weekend to close out my apartment.

Packer tickets were easy to come by in Detroit so I took the chance to see an indoor NFL football game at the Pontiac Silverdome. It seemed the Packers had more fans there than the Lions. They definitely were the ones tailgating. I had purchased 3 tickets hoping my brother Jim and nephew Scott could go. That did not work out, so I ended up selling two of them at cost. It took over an hour at the gate, when finally some Packer fans came to my rescue. A story circulating in Detroit had this guy with two tickets to a Lions game which he didn't want to go to because the team was doing so poorly. On a trip to the grocery store, he put both tickets under his windshield wipers hoping some one would take them. Lo and behold, when he returned back to his vehicle after shopping, two more tickets were added to his.

Later in October, I attended my nephew Scott and Traci's wedding in Ann Arbor. It was an occasion when much of the family from Wisconsin attended. We had a nice reunion. By Christmas, my assignment was finished at GM so I motored to Wisconsin to spend the holidays with family.

CHAPTER XVI

GAMING EDUCATION

Before the new year of 1998 started, I was back in Arizona living off my contract pay for three months. I kept busy with some travel to Edwards AFB to visit Brian who was stationed there at that time. My sister Nancy got married in Estes Park, Colorado in March requiring a trip to Denver. I drove to Tucson to fly with my Uncle Clarence and Aunt Marie who also attended the occasion. They were not accustomed to flying so I took the opportunity to travel with them. I enjoyed our big reunion with family in the Rockies.

An opportunity soon opened up for me at the Ramada Resort in Laughlin. This Financial Analyst position was an experience somewhat related to my engineering background but was only temporary until a CPA could be located. After returning to Laughlin, it was time to start my job at Ramada which gave me an opportunity to see all the stage shows first hand. My job was to analyze the revenue generated by these concerts against the cost. It was always exciting to see and sometimes meet these entertainers even though they were past their prime in the show business.

During the football season, it was routine to watch Monday Night Football at the Golden Nugget in the lounge with friends. The beverage prices were right and they had lots of door prizes whenever a team scored. One such prize I received was for a trip on the Grand Canyon Railway for two. Again I rode the rail this time with Christine. By the end of the year, I was becoming quite informed as to how the resort and gaming industry subsisted.

With my time at Ramada certain changes in my equilibrium were becoming part of my life. It wasn't going to be until several years later I'd discover the cause. Maybe it was just self denial or maybe age creeping up on me so I learned to live with it. A visit to a chiropractor for stiffness in the upper body seemed to help somewhat. Physically all was fine for the most part. I gave job stress most of the blame.

As usual, the weekends typically required a road trip somewhere, but not alone. In January, Christine and I drove to Algadones, Baja California, Mexico for a shopping trip and just a get-a-way with a night spent in Yuma, Arizona. It was always exciting to venture into Mexico for bargains and a good margarita. When mom and dad came out again in March, I had to give them an adventure to that Desert Bar near Parker. This was always a thrill for me as well as any guests that might have ridden along.

By April, it was getting warm enough for a trip up to the 'Valley of Fire' just Northeast of Las Vegas which I wanted to see for quite sometime. My friend Christine and I took a nice leisurely drive on Lake Mead Drive Boulevard past Lake Las Vegas to this scenic State Park. The colors were gorgeous and the hikes were very exhilarating. I still remember very vividly, Christine climbing up this rocky terrace to have her picture taken. Well, it was a nice picture, but, as I warned her, it is always more difficult coming back down. She did rather well until the last 50 feet or so. One foot didn't want to go where she wanted it to go and then she started tumbling until she hit a huge boulder with her head. I believe I felt it more than she. But she was ok......hurrah! The tumble just injured her pride somewhat. That night we headed back to Vegas and stayed at Sunrise Suites on Boulder highway before heading back to Laughlin on Sunday. Later in June 1999, my sister Kathy, Bob, the 3 boys, Brandon, Tony and Joe made a drive out to Laughlin from Wisconsin to view some of the beautiful National Parks we have in the Southwest. I did take them on a day trip up to Hoover Dam which impressed them enough to talk about it for a long time afterward.

Now it was getting toward the end of summer and daughter Brenda was in need of her dad to present her in marriage over in Maui. It was just a 3 day trip because I had my class reunion yet also in September. I only had 2 weeks when I got back to Laughlin from Hawaii before I left again for Wisconsin. Our 35th reunion was in Door County which is probably one of the more beautiful places in the state. That again was a short trip because I had trouble making my vacation reach the whole year. By year end, my employer was ready for the recently hired accountant to take over the work load I had and I was released of my temporary duties. About 4 months prior, I was informed that he would be taking over those duties so I had been actively searching for possibilities that would keep me in the Southwest.

CHAPTER XVII

NEW MILLENIUM -
ANOTHER SPEED BUMP

Most of us will remember the time when we were in an undetermined state as to what happens when the clock strikes midnight to welcome in the year 2000. The whole world as we know it was coming to an end as a few people thought. But, like any other new year, it was just another new year like I anticipated it to be.

As I was searching for employment after my departure from Ramada Express, my mom and dad had driven out to Nevada for their annual winter get-a-way. We prearranged a weekend visit to Fresno to visit relatives with a stop in California City to see Brian. This visit also led Larry and Doreen to come down from Calistoga to join us so we had a partial family reunion in Fresno. Our cousin Father Rod solemnized the church services on Sunday. He informed us of more relatives in the area. The return trip included more stops to see relatives that we didn't know we had. The night was spent in Tehachapi which is surrounded by thousands of power generating wind turbines and is also noted for being the world's largest producer of wind energy. Upon our return to my condo in Laughlin, they continued their drive back to enjoy the friendly confines of winter as it was waning away.

I thought my efforts of submitting numerous resumes were starting to pay off as I was invited to fly down to Tucson and also up to Reno for job interviews. But, after these trips, nothing materialized and I would then accept a position back at Leupp to assist with the electronic manufacturing business. Now, I had to squeeze in my pre-planned trip to Wisconsin before I got down to serious work. It was during this trip, my nephew Scott and his wife Tracey from Michigan and I attended a Packer preseason scrimmage in Green Bay. It was our fate that we got to chat with Brett Favre after practice.

Now it was toward the end of August on my return to Arizona and my first day at Tooh Dineh. It was nice to see all my past associates once again. This time I shortened my commute by 20 miles one way by taking up residence in Winslow even though it didn't have the amenities of Flagstaff. My first month, I lodged in several motels that had weekly rates until in October I located a so-called apartment. Two rooms joined in a converted motel was OK as I didn't plan on living in Winslow until retirement. But the town was somewhat warmer and we didn't get snow only once or twice a winter. I believe about two or three weekends were spent in Winslow and generally my weekends were spent in Flagstaff to have somewhat of a social life. That guy was still 'standing on the corner' when I lived there. Remember the Eagles song "Take it Easy" from the '70s?

I did get to see my step-grandson from Laughlin in a football game in Williams. About every 6 weeks when the weather complied, I did manage a trip to Laughlin where the climate was much more suitable. Our traditional plant shutdown for the Christmas holidays allowed me to spend time in Laughlin to get out of the cold.

After the first of the year, my health was now becoming an issue. I really didn't have an explanation whether it be job stress or maybe just despondency. As time moved onwards, my days were long and tiring with headaches. By March 2001, I decided something must be done, so I talked with the General Manager and informed him that I would have to resign to evaluate what the problem might be. In my final week of work, my mind was already somewhere else and I needed some time away. A nephew Mason and his cousin Peter stopped by in Winslow for a visit on their way to San Diego. They didn't find me standing on the corner either, as I was in no condition to do so as they found out.

During this unstable period of time I vacated my apartment in Winslow and drove to Henderson to stay with a friend. This was already April so I decided to take a trip to Maui to spend some time with Brenda. My condition improved somewhat by being away from work but not back to normal. The three weeks with Brenda on Maui and a trip over to the Big Island was a boost. Several meetings were scheduled in Hilo for possible opportunities in the future with acquaintances I garnered when living there before. I guess the possibilities were strong but something told me to hold off at that time. I returned to Henderson the end of April and then drove down to Laughlin to get my mail from the Post Office box that I rented there. This was because of my chaos in my present life and indecision where I was headed. I spent a couple weeks in Henderson with my friend Christine. In the middle of May I drove over to Edwards AFB to spend a week with Brian. We took in a minor league baseball game in Lancaster where we met my nephews Mason and Jon and niece Caryn with their friends. A good time was had considering my circumstances.

In June I'm still wondering what is going on and needed to find some employment to meet expenses. There was always something that lingered as to why not at this time. The end of June came and I flew back to Wisconsin to visit family for 2 weeks. Because of another nephew Barry getting an award at school, he was entitled to choose someone to accompany him at Road America June Sprints in the Pace car before the race. So Barry got to ride in the lead car and I followed in the 2nd Pace car. Of course, we didn't drive but it was very exciting being strapped in this race car going around this curvy four mile track at 60 MPH. By mid July I flew back to Las Vegas and by August a voice told me something was still in a state of uncertainty. I then told Christine I would be driving back to Wisconsin for some unknown reason at that time. On Friday morning at 6 am, I'm on my way and Sunday afternoon I was at mom and dad's house. How I ever made that trip alone had to be under the guidance of our dear Lord.

This time my family became more aware of my situation. They then made some necessary moves to find possible causes of my condition. After a visit with the family doctor, I was immediately scheduled for an MRI (Magnetic Resonance Imaging) in Chilton. Dr. Pleviak, from these results, was suspect of what was the likely cause of my condition and scheduled me for a visit with a highly recommended neurosurgeon at Theda Clark Medical Center in Neenah, Wisconsin. When the negatives were displayed on Dr. Lyons' lighted viewer he pointed out the trouble spot. My heart sank down to the floor. I thought this can't be again! This tumor was 4 centimeters in size like a golf ball. He explained, the cause was from the radiation treatments I received in 1963 for the tumor I had removed at that time. So what is the next move and what options do I have, I ask? He informed me that thing has to come out of there and scheduled me for surgery 4 days later. I didn't have a whole lot of time to think about what was about to happen and maybe for the better. I called my daughter Brenda and my son Brian that night and told them I was in good hands and not to worry. I guess I was in a daze for the next 4 days because I don't remember much in detail. Brenda showed up with her husband Ed at mom and dad's door the day before surgery and Brian was there the morning of. Never did I expect either of them, nor did I want them to travel so many miles just for this minor inconvenience or another speed bump in my life. Brian's wife Suk and son Min also made the trip from Nevada and made me wonder what this commotion was all about.

On September 6, I was driven to Theda Clark for surgery. I could have driven myself and left the car there for a day or two. My day was very short but very long for those in the waiting area outside of surgery. I remember going into that operating room at 8:30 AM hoping that Dr. Lyons didn't have bowling the night before and the next thing I remember is being wheeled out of surgery at 4:30 pm. Discharge was on September 11th the same day this country had that rude awakening. This day will always be on my mind and I'm very thankful my surgery didn't take place on that day because no one could concentrate on what they were doing.

A special distinction clings to a neurosurgeon because they tinker with the part of us that makes us who we are. Many times we have heard the expression in conversation, 'I'm not a brain surgeon' which probably means we are not on that same intelligence level.

The next several months were lackluster as I was rehabilitating myself so I could proceed with unfinished business, meaning I had places to go. Brenda stayed with me on the homestead for three weeks to help me adjust with the cold weather setting in. Without her I would have had a much more difficult time with the whole program. Before she left for home in Kauai, she informed me, "if the winter gets to old for me, I should spend some time with her and Ed". Well, by time winter started, it was too much already and plans were made for the trip across the water by end of

January. In November I had the pleasure of a surprise party on the 16th. It was the 17th anniversary of my 39th birthday and was attended by about 20 family members at Millhome Supper Club. Later, on Christmas Day, after the festive atmosphere was slipping away, I left for West Bend with my sister Ellen, Tom and Katrina for a house sitting job while they went to Australia for three weeks. This was very relaxing. It gave me time to meditate on the many speed bumps we all have in life. Some slow you down more than others!

It was only Gizzy the cat and me, except for one day when we had a 50th birthday party with family for Ellen even though she wasn't there. After a couple weeks the cat even came to trust me. Can you image that? They returned on the 16th of January and the next day I returned to the homestead to make ready for my trip to Kauai.

CHAPTER XVIII

RETURN TO ECSTASY

After my post-operative visit with Dr. Lyons on January 21st, my departure was approved. One day later, without much reluctance, my brother Roger and I left in my Outback for California. With overnight stops in Rolla, MO, Tucumcari, NM, Laughlin, NV and Delano, CA we were soon in Calistoga by my brother Larry. I spent the next week with them while Roger flew back to Wisconsin to enjoy the winter for a while. During this next week I made arrangements to ship my car to Kauai because I owed more than it was worth. Selling it was not an option. Larry and I spent a day over in Bodega Bay for some time to talk while watching the surf. Mr. Hitchcock and the seagulls were no longer a problem as they were several decades ago in the movie.

On February 9th I was met at the airport in Lihue by Brenda. The air certainly did feel good. After I got settled in their house, two days later Roger, Cathy and their friends arrived on a preplanned trip for five days. Our time together was minimal as I was still getting adjusted and their friends occupied most of the time they had. I had an almost daily routine, where I rode to work with Brenda and then walked back home a little over 2 miles for exercise. In my leisure time I volunteered as a greeter when passengers disembarked from the weekly cruise ships that docked in Lihue. It was always interesting to observe the big ships as they maneuvered out of the small harbor. As time past to April, I flew over to Maui to see my friend Lucy as it had been several years since the last visit. She had just turned 90 in March and was able to get around yet with her Malibu Chevy. When returning to Kauai, I did find some temporary work to keep me out of trouble and pay some bills.

Brother Larry and an associate Javier from work flew over for a week to soak up some sun. Larry's wife Doreen wasn't home anyhow at that time. She was on an educational and pleasure trip in Ireland so what else could Larry do? They had a breathtaking time hiking various parts of the island that I can only dream about and will never see up close. My summer was adventuresome and in September I flew to Las Vegas for five days for a reunion with mom and dad for their 59th anniversary. We met with my brother Roger, his wife Cathy and son Jon, my brother Larry and wife Doreen for a special and good time.

October I started an assignment with Hale Kauai, Ltd which was in business as a building supply company. My job entailed some retail sales but mostly using

AutoCad and kitchen layout software on the computer for the home planning department. It was interesting work but also quite stressful because the contractors always needed the plans with a very short turnaround time. They were made aware of my situation before hire. It was on a trial basis. It was a great group of people to work with and was always an enjoyment to go to work. Christmas Eve was a half day at work and the company had a party at Kalapaki Beach with plenty to drink and lots of octopus on the grill. New Year's Eve, I was my old self and commemorated the coming New Year by means of being in bed by 10 pm.

In January, I had my annual MRI to observe any differences that may have occurred and was informed by the neurologist all looks as it was before the surgery minus the trouble spot of course. This was a weight off my mind and lifted my spirits immensely. Now I could enjoy my time with Roger who again was to arrive for his winter get-a-way. After all, watching the Super Bowl would not be the same without him at Nawiliwili tavern in Lihue down by the harbor. We squeezed in as much activity in the 2 weeks that the brutal weather would allow compared to the nice weather back in Wisconsin.

Volunteering with NOAA (National Oceanic & Atmospheric Administration) for their annual humpback whale survey was a highlight for me in February and March. This event is scheduled the last Saturday of the month and is quite accurate by the means they use throughout the Islands simultaneously to prevent any duplication of counts. This was achieved by groups of 2 to 8 volunteers located strategically around the 5 major islands in Hawaii. When the count was finished, we were invited to Kilauea Point National Wildlife Refuge to observe an albatross colony that was off limits to the general public. These birds are huge and awkward. They need a short runway to take flight and are usually gone for several days to fetch food for their single hatchling. Anyhow, it was a rewarding experience for the hours we volunteered to just sit on the beach and watch over the blue sea for whales.

April came and now I had another one week assignment of house-sitting for Brenda and Ed while they ventured off to the mainland for vacation. By now the cats, (Babu, Kahlua and Sylvester) knew where their food was coming from so they had a lot of respect for me and that made the job a piece of cake. They knew they wouldn't live on geckos alone. By mid-summer we had Dori and Jim come for a much needed vacation after their son was involved in an auto accident in April. One of the adventures we took was a tubing trip down an old abandoned sugar flume. It was hand dug by plantation workers during the 1800s to send the harvested cane down the mountain to the refinery. The flumes didn't go over the mountains but rather through the mountains to maintain the downward flow of the water from the mountains above. These hand dug tunnels (some of which were almost a 1 mile in length) were navigated with hardhats with lights. They were similar to a miner's helmet. In the middle, neither opening was visible. At the end of our excursion, all participants were accounted for and lunch was provided by our guides.

Another day was set aside for a 5 hour snorkel cruise with Capt. Andy's charter service. Snorkeling in 50 feet of water for someone with little swimming experience at first caused some hesitation. Our guide and captain soon reassured us. Sneeki Tikis for drinks and pupus for a snack being the mainstay of the afternoon while we took in some of the most spectacular sights in Hawaii along the Na Pali coast. Edging our catamaran into some of the sea caves and also seeing waterfalls that are not visible from land made this excursion the highlight of my time with them on Kauai. Their time on Kauai was pretty much non-stop fun even with the geckos under Dori's pillow. Jim had a difficult time understanding the language of the many feral chickens roaming the island. It never failed when a rooster would cross the road in front of us, he would cock-a-doodle-doo to the hen he left behind. Well, if you listen closely, he was actually telling her "you can do it too", insinuating, I made it, why can't you? After a short course in chicken language for Jim, we fed those scoundrels one last time before they headed to the airport for their long flight home to Wisconsin.

I resigned from my job at the computer reluctantly due to recurrent headaches caused by anxiety. I took up residence back on the mainland with Brian and Suk in Las Vegas for a while and left Brenda and Ed to manage with the cats alone.

Though we all have our speed bumps in life, they are meant to keep us from getting bored with our existence. They may slow us down enough to become a directional guide in life. We have to pay attention to these subtle signs and ask for help from God to differentiate between our needs and wants.

My dreams continue to this day and I saw many come true. I've come to realize the most important things in life, are not material things. Sometimes it's good to pause in our search for happiness and just be happy.

ABOUT THE AUTHOR

Ron J. Woelfel is a native of Wisconsin and grew up on a small farm in Calumet County. He attended catholic schools in New Holstein, St. Nazianz and several technical schools in Wisconsin as well as universities in Wisconsin, Arizona and Hawaii. His life as a farm boy and work as Industrial Engineer has taken him many places in the Southwest and Hawaiian Islands. By working in Wisconsin, Mexico, Hawaii and on the Navajo Reservation in Arizona, he has come to appreciate many cultures during his life. The people, cities, national parks and many other breathtaking scenic outdoor places have filled his life with enchantment. He currently resides in Nevada and part-time on Kauai with family.